MASHA KOSOVSKAYA • ALLA TYAKHT • DMITRY ALEXEE

TIM'S
ADVENTURES
IN THE WORLD
OF BACTERIA

Dedication

To our friend Tim and all our kids,
whose endless curiosity is an inspiration for us.

Thank you Tim, for helping us in translation.

And to the "Little Tim" inside every one of us,
a child which never stops exploring and
is able to set forth on dangerous
adventures in the name of love.

Don't forget to hug your Mom – they say it is the best medicine!

CONTENTS

It all started with a microscope — 2

How bacteria appeared — 4

Not all microbes are bacteria — 8

The immunity and wet feet — 10

Mom's got an infection — 12

At Dad's lab — 14

Bacterium structure — 18

Bacterial reproduction — 20

Bacteria plating — 22

How Tim met Bacteroid — 24

At the bacteria party — 26

Evolution — 28

Charles Darwin — 30

At the hospital — 32

Air — 34

Bacteria in water — 36

Soil — 38

The natural cycle of matter — 40

The biological cycle — 42

Extremophiles — 44

Bacteria rule the world — 46

Bacteria inside a human body — 48

A journey inside — 50

In the throat — 52

Esophagus — 54

Stomach — 56

Duodenum — 58

The digestion factory: small intestine — 60

Dad has had lunch — 62

Intestinal immunity — 64

The appendix is a dead end — 66

Large Intestines, Bacteria Metropolises — 68

Healthy food — 70

Unhealthy food — 72

Intestinal mafia — 74

At the festival — 76

Microorganisms at the service of the human body — 80

Salmonella attack — 82

Horizontal transfer — 84

Slenderness city — 86

Fartsville — 88

Bacterial rap battle — 90

Mom's recovery — 94

IT ALL STARTED WITH A MICROSCOPE

One day Dad gave Tim a microscope.
Tim looked inside it and saw strange tiny creatures.

Dad! What are these?

Those are bacteria.

A MICROSCOPE is a device to closely examine the tiniest objects. For example, specks of dust are very tiny. But you can see them when they float in the air in a beam of sunlight. With a microscope you can take a closer look at things that are much smaller than specks of dust. A microscope magnifies objects with the help of lenses. They are called **MAGNIFYING GLASSES**. Lenses can refract light.

HANDS-ON

Pour some water into a glass and put a spoon inside. If you look from the side, the spoon will look like it is broken and has got bigger. It happens because water refracts light.

Scientists use the refraction effect with some lenses and mirrors to make a MICROSCOPE.

BACTERIA – are microorganisms (also known as germs).

MICROORGANISMS are living things, so small you can't see them without a microscope. Under the microscope, they look like beads, rods, or beans with tails.

There are other microorganisms beside bacteria, such as mold, yeast and protozoa. We'll talk about them later, but for now let's get back to bacteria.

Take a look around. Wherever you look is home to bacteria. That's right! For example, there are millions of them on your palm. If we get that many mice and put them into train cars, the'll fill an entire train.

But where do they come from, if you wash your hands every day?

You have touched different things:
- the elevator button,
- a ball on the street,
- the coin you picked up from the sidewalk.

All of these objects had bacteria that migrated to your hands. By the way, when you shake someone's hand, the bacteria move from your hand to your friend's hand, and vice versa.

The words "microscope" and "microorganism" have the part "micro" in them, which means "very, very small."

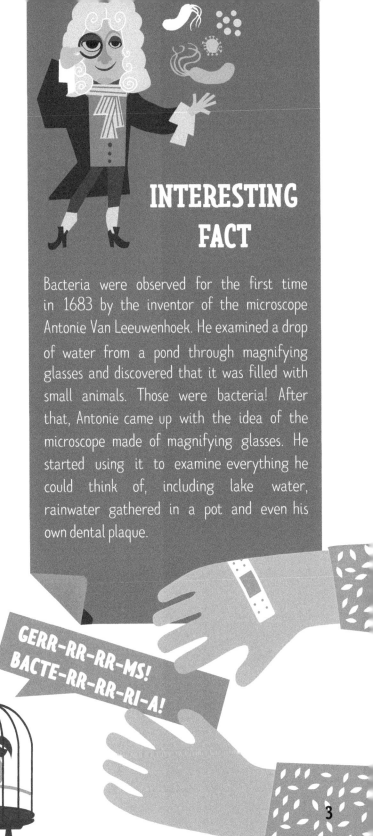

INTERESTING FACT

Bacteria were observed for the first time in 1683 by the inventor of the microscope Antonie Van Leeuwenhoek. He examined a drop of water from a pond through magnifying glasses and discovered that it was filled with small animals. Those were bacteria! After that, Antonie came up with the idea of the microscope made of magnifying glasses. He started using it to examine everything he could think of, including lake water, rainwater gathered in a pot and even his own dental plaque.

GERR-RR-RR-MS! BACTE-RR-RR-RI-A!

3

HOW BACTERIA APPEARED

Bacteria appeared on Earth a very long time ago, around 3 or 4 billion years ago. At that time, our planet didn't have any plants, or animals, let alone people. Bacteria, or rather archaebacteria, the ancestors of modern bacteria, were the first living things on Earth.

A SCIENTIFIC HYPOTHESIS is a guess or an idea scientists have about something. For example, about where bacteria came from to Earth. If scientists manage to find proof and conduct experiments to confirm their guess, then the hypothesis turns into a theory.

Dad, where did bacteria come from?

That's a very good question. The thing is, scientists don't know for sure. But they have two hypotheses.

Meteorites and asteroids are chunks of rock and ice, moving in outer space and sometimes falling down to Earth.

Hypothesis 1

Bacteria came from outer space

According to the first hypothesis, bacteria came from outer space. Not in a rocket like astronauts, but on meteorites and asteroids that fell to Earth.

COMETS consist of rock, ice and gas. If a comet passes close to the Sun, it appears to have a "tail."

ASTEROIDS are huge chunks of rock. They can be as big as the Moon. If an asteroid ever collides with the Earth, there could be a huge catastrophe. For example, according to one hypothesis, dinosaurs were wiped out by a big asteroid that hit our planet.

After METEOROIDS hit Earth, they turn into METEROITES. Meteorites are smaller than asteroids, the size of big or small rocks. Sometimes we see shooting stars in the sky: those are rocks that come from space and burn up in the Earth's atmosphere. They are also called METEORS.

The first ancient bacteria must have been so happy to come to Earth! After an endless voyage through space, they finally found a home!

HYPOTHESIS 2

Primordial soup

According to the other hypothesis, bacteria appeared all by themselves in the primordial ocean of our planet. Scientists refer to the water, where life originated, as the primordial soup. Just like carrots, potatoes and meat boil in a regular soup, complex molecules of different substances floated in the primordial soup and gradually connected to each other like puzzle pieces until they formed a living bacterium.

There is another hypothesis called the primordial soup. It must have been cooked by a primordial parent.

THEORR-RR-RRY! PRRRIMOR-RRR-DIAL SOUP!

Any matter consists of tiny particles, i.e. **MOLECULES.**

A molecule is built of even smaller "building blocks." They are called **ATOMS**.

ATOMS are small indivisible particles. Well, it is actually possible to divide them, but it's really hard. If left alone, atoms can get bored. They join into groups and form molecules.

Molecules may be complex, i.e. include a lot of atoms.

Neither atoms nor molecules are **LIVING ORGANISMS.**

A BACTERIUM is a living organism. It eats and grows like you, and after it's all grown up, it starts reproducing.

Scientists still don't know how exactly molecules, even very complex ones, finally formed a living bacterium. That was a real miracle! Imagine if you'd made a bit of dough out of water, eggs and flour, and it suddenly jumped down from the kitchen table and ran away.

NOT ALL MICROBES ARE BACTERIA

Are microbes and bacteria the same?

All microorganisms are called microbes.

Microorganisms, or microbes, have lived on Earth much longer than humans. It wasn't them who moved in with us. We, humans, came to their world.

Microorganisms are protozoa, bacteria, some fungi and viruses. Viruses, however, aren't fully functional organisms. The study of microorganisms is called **MICROBIOLOGY.**

INTERESTING FACT

The word "microbe" was invented by the French scientist Émile Littré at the request of scientist Charles Sédillot. Littré just added the letters "BE" to the word "MICRO" to get the funny word "microbe."

Let's tell you about different types of microbes:

PROTOZOA are the smallest animals. They have a more complex structure but are still too small to see with the naked eye.

There are different types of **FUNGI**. Some of them, such as many mushrooms, are edible. Other kinds include yeast and mold.

You have surely seen **MOLD** many times. It grows on old bread that has been kept in a plastic bag for a long time. Tiny mold particles are always floating in the air, looking for something to eat. As soon as they find anything suitable, they start reproducing, forming white, green or black spots — colonies.

OOPS!

Looks like I'm fermenting!

VIRUSES are a distinct group of microorganisms. We can't say that they are fully alive, because they can only live inside bacteria or other organisms. They can't survive in the environment by themselves.

Some viruses are at war with the bacteria. Those viruses that are able to kill the bacteria are called BACTERIOPHAGES.

YEAST are fungi too, but unlike mold, they prefer a liquid environment. If apple juice starts bubbling up and tastes weird, that means it started FERMENTING.

Fermenting means that bacteria or yeasts started multiplying in the liquid. During fermentation, they start chemical reactions that release a lot of gas. Bakers often add yeast to dough to make bread soft and full of air bubbles. You have to keep an eye on the dough, though.
If you don't, it may rise too high over the rim of the pan.

A multitude of bacteria live in the human body like in a house. Everyone of us is home to about ten trillion bacteria! That's a lot. That's more than there are people on Earth! Imagine: you are a planet for bacteria.

TEN TRILLION LOOKS LIKE THIS — 10 000 000 000 000!

If we weigh all the bacteria living inside you, scales will indicate 200g (7 oz). That's how muc glass of milk weighs.

Mom, if it were my feet that got wet, why did my throat start hurting? It should be my feet!

You got too chilled! That's why your immunity has decreased.

IMMUNITY is the body's ability to protect us from viruses.

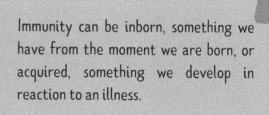

Immunity can be inborn, something we have from the moment we are born, or acquired, something we develop in reaction to an illness.

Microbes are important for our health. The bacteria that inhabit our body protect us from various harmful bacteria, help us digest our food, produce some vitamins and maintain our immune system. In other words, they are doing their best to be helpful to us. However, this huge crowd that lives inside us needs to be kept on a leash, otherwise, some of them can get where they are not supposed to.

Our immune system balances the microbes inhabiting our body with the body itself. Immune cells safeguard our immune system, just like tiny police officers. They fight harmful microbes that might make their way inside our body by catching and destroying them.

ICR-R-R-OBE

If you're wearing wet shoes outside for a long time, your body needs to spend a lot of energy to keep you warm. That energy is diverted from your immune system, so it becomes less efficient. The police officers get lazy or skip work completely. That is why we say that your immune system has been compromised.

If your immune system is weakened, even the "good" bacteria might start acting against you. And if germs get inside your body, you are going to get sick for sure. Your immune system might be weakened if you get too cold, lack sleep, keep to an unhealthy diet, have vitamin deficiency, or just a bad mood.

MOM'S GOT AN INFECTION

INTERESTING FACT

INFECTION is a word derived from Lat[in]. Infectious diseases are caused by m[i]crobes and viruses, which get inside human body.

What happened to Mom? Why was she taken to the hospital?

She got sick. She has an infection.

INFE-E-ECTION!

The immunity pushes back bad bacteria that get into your body. But sometimes it fails and the invaders settle down in your throat, lungs, intestines or on your skin.

A common cold is usually a piece of cake for your immunity. But bacteria can cause more serious diseases like scarlet fever, whooping cough, tetanus, tuberculosis and many others which can only be treated by a doctor.

Bad bacteria can get into your body with dirty food, bad water or with air (when a sick person sneezes or coughs near you). Most of the time bacteria end up on your hands and then travel to your nose or mouth. That's why it's so important to wash your hands.

When a person gets sick, a war starts inside of them and the immunity troops gather on the battlefield. For each type of bacteria the immunity has to find the right weapon. This weapon is called ANTIBODIES.

While the immunity is looking for the right antibodies, just like for the right key to a lock, we feel sick. Once the antibodies are found, we feel better. We say we've developed immunity to the disease. But in order for the immunity to develop we have to get sick and then get well. But some diseases are very dangerous and can be deadly. What should we do then?

Before vaccination was invented, EPIDEMICS were a common occurrence. An epidemic is when many people die from infectious diseases.

INTERESTING FACT

Scientists invented VACCINATION. A person is given an injection with a little bit of fluid containing microbes – the vaccine. These microbes are very weak and cannot hurt you. But they can teach the immunity to tackle really dangerous microbes.

The first shot was given by Doctor Edward Jenner in 1796. Little by little they started vaccinating everybody against various diseases. Thanks to these shots many dangerous diseases disappeared.

"A plague doctor" was a physician who treated plague. He wore a mask with a beak shaped nose stuffed with medicine, the smell of which was supposed to protect the doctor from getting infected.

AT DAD'S LAB

The next day Tim was very upset about Mom's illness. So Dad decided to take Tim to work with him. Tim was happy. He'd finally learn what a real laboratory looks like!

Labs can be SCIENTIFIC and MEDICAL. Medical labs are for medical tests. When you get a blood test in a hospital, your blood is taken to a medical lab to find out whether you are sick. Scientific labs are places to conduct experiments, invent medicines and make discoveries. Tim's dad is a microbiologist. A microbiologist studies MICROORGANISMS. A microbiologist's lab is similar to a medical one, except it has more complicated devices.

DNA, or deoxyribonucleic acid, is a superlong molecule containing encoded information about the way a living being functions.

Tangled cables hide the name of a friendly bacterium, can you read it?

Dad's lab has a very complex DNA sequencer, which is a very recent invention.

With a supercomputer, it deciphers this information and tells us what properties a microbe has.

This is a CLUSTER, a supercomputer built of a number of high-performance computers. It can run many complex computing operations simultaneously and quickly.

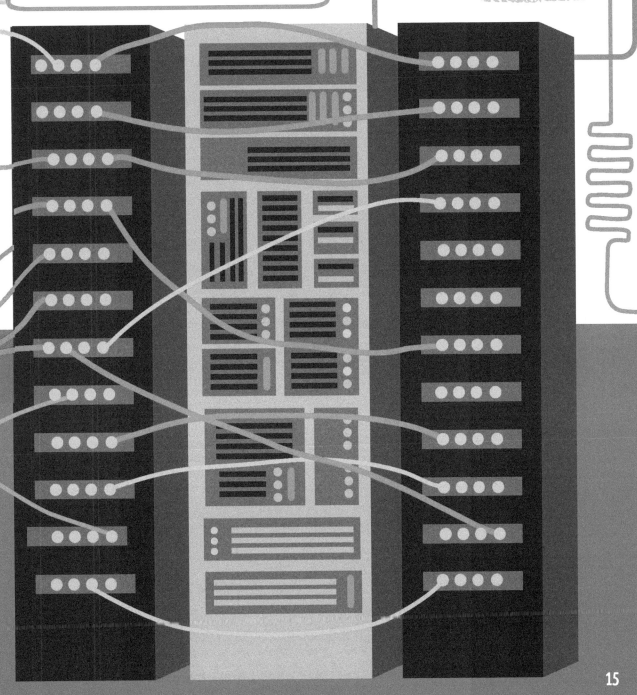

AT DAD'S LAB

A LAB REACTOR is a device where chemical reactions take place. A chemical reaction is when several chemical substances are mixed. They dissociate into fragments which then come together to form new molecules. This way one substance turns into another.

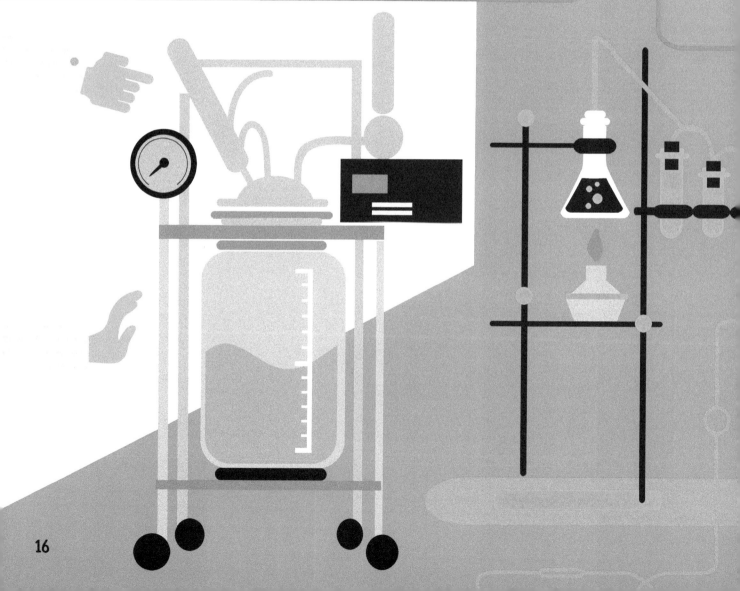

An ELECTRONIC MICROSCOPE magnifies things using electricity and magnetic lenses instead of glass ones. An electronic microscope can zoom something a million times. A hair magnified like this will look like a 12-story building.

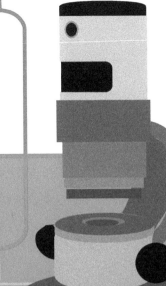

Every modern laboratory has a COMPUTER. Scientists use computers to store and analyze data obtained during their experiments.

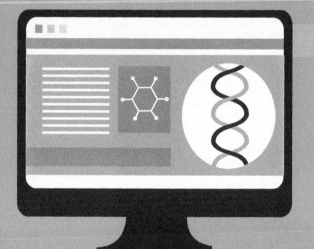

A LABORATORY CENTRIFUGE is used to analyze various substances. Test tubes are placed in the centrifuge. Then it rotates very fast. The rotation helps divide the material into liquid and pellet (stuff that settles on the bottom).

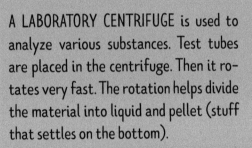

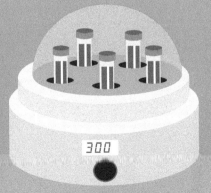

300

BACTERIUM STRUCTURE

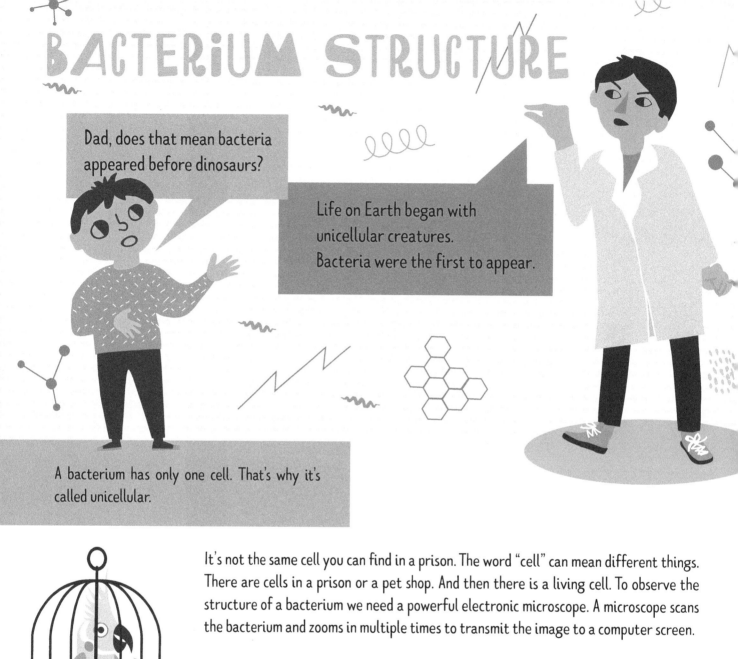

Dad, does that mean bacteria appeared before dinosaurs?

Life on Earth began with unicellular creatures. Bacteria were the first to appear.

A bacterium has only one cell. That's why it's called unicellular.

It's not the same cell you can find in a prison. The word "cell" can mean different things. There are cells in a prison or a pet shop. And then there is a living cell. To observe the structure of a bacterium we need a powerful electronic microscope. A microscope scans the bacterium and zooms in multiple times to transmit the image to a computer screen.

MEMBR-R-RANE!

A bacterium is wrapped in a tough envelope. This is the CELL WALL that protects it and gives it shape.

18

A BACTERIUM CONSISTS OF ONE CELL.
Let's take a closer look.

Some bacteria have **MEMBRANES** under their cell walls. A membrane is a smart layer that lets the good substances in while squeezing harmful ones out. This process is called **METABOLISM.**

Every living organism – plants, animals, birds, and, of course, people – consists of cells. Your entire body is a collection of minuscule living things. Each cell is an individual organism that eats, grows and reproduces itself.

All living organisms are divided into single-celled or multicellular.

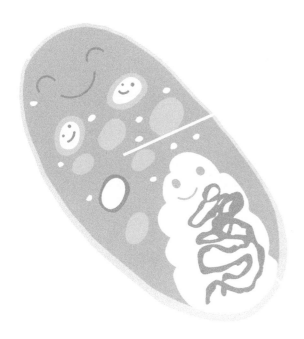

A cell has a special liquid inside called CYTOPLASM.

Cytoplasm is water with mineral salts and glucose (sugar) dissolved in it. It also contains various complex molecules.

The most important part of a bacterium is found in its center. It's DNA, and it looks like a knot of small worms. The DNA is like an encyclopedia that has all the information about the bacterium: what it is, what it eats, how it grows and reproduces, how many flagella it has, where it likes to live. (Do you remember Dad's laboratory with the DNA-reading machine?)

Some bacteria have hair-like **PILI** and lash-like **FLAGELLA.** They help the bacteria move and interact.

Also, bacteria have ribosomes, vacuoles and other complex molecules. Like gears in a machine, they are always working, and that's how a bacterium lives.

BACTERIAL REPRODUCTION

A bacterium doesn't have a mom or a dad. It reproduces by fission. That means a bacterium splits itself in two equal halves. First, everything inside the bacteria is split in half, and then these halves go in opposite directions. After that, the cell is split down the middle. We get two cells just like the original one, but smaller. Then they grow up and split again. Now, there are 4 of them.

You already know what reproduction means, don't you?

That's when living things have children. Cats give birth to kittens, dogs have puppies and humans have babies. Bacteria don't give birth to anyone, they split into halves!

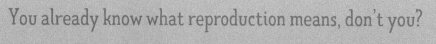

I wish people could do the same. I would split myself in two to have someone to play with.

That would certainly be great. But if you could do that like bacteria, there would be too many Tims.

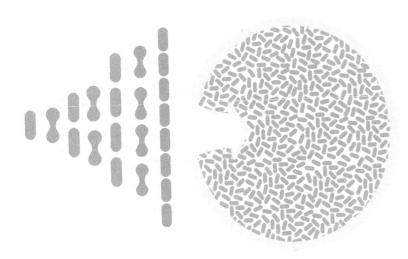

Bacteria divide very quickly, approximately once every 20 minutes. In a day, one bacterium can produce about 5000 quintillion new ones – those are thousands of billions of billions of bacteria. All together they would weigh as much as one adult elephant! If bacteria always had enough to eat, they would take over the whole planet in just a day and a half! There would be no room left for people.

As long as bacteria have food, they reproduce and build colonies. Bacterial colonies are, in fact, just one bacterium that has reproduced. But, once the food runs out, the colony dies. Also, direct sunlight, drying, warming up, detergents and disinfectants kill most bacteria.

SPOR-R-RES!
R-R-EPRODUCTION!

INTERESTING FACT

In order to survive, some bacteria turn into SPORES. A bacterium dries out and falls sound asleep like Sleeping Beauty. Spores are more resistant to adverse conditions, but they do not reproduce and just wait to be rescued and kissed by Prince Charming. Just kidding. Spores wait for favorable conditions, when they will be able to come to life and turn into bacterium again.

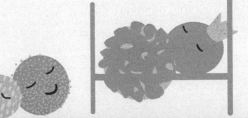

BACTERIA PLATING

We can try and find bacterium responsible for Mom's illness. In order to do that let's conduct an experiment.

A PETRI DISH is a flat glass jar filled with nutritious jelly. Some bacteria are placed inside and covered with a lid. Bacteria eat the nutrient jelly and reproduce. After a while bacterial colonies grow so much that they become visible to the naked eye. By the look of a colony you can tell what bacteria it is made up of.

To identify the type of bacteria we use **PLATING**. That is when we plate something and then it grows. Like planting seeds into the ground. Bacteria are plated onto special nutrient jelly into a **PETRI DISH**.

The nutritious environment for bacteria is made of agar-agar. That is a substance obtained from seaweed and used to make jelly. In order for the bacteria colony to grow some broth is usually added to the solution. Chicken broth, for example. Bacteria love it.

HANDS-ON

Prepare three Petri dishes (you can order them on-line) and make nutritious environments for the bacteria (one glass of chicken broth and 2 teaspoons of agar-agar). Let the solution cool, then lift up the lid of the Petri dish a little, pour the solution in and put the lid back on.

You have to wait for the solution to cool completely to plate some bacteria. Then, swab your palm with a cotton ball and streak the bacteria to the agar in dish #1.

Put a piece of tape on it and label it "hand". Take another cotton ball to swab your your phone and make a plating. Put some tape on this one, too, and label it "phone." Use the third cotton ball to swab the sole of your shoe and streak it into dish #3. Label this plating as "shoe".

Bacteria plating helps us identify if the person has angina, tuberculosis or other diseases caused by bacteria.

PLATING is a test performed by medical labs.

PHONE   HAND

SHOE

Set the plating jars aside in a warm place for 5 – 7 days. Watch your colonies grow. Take pictures of them every day. Describe the colonies. Which of them are alike and which are different? Draw a conclusion from your experiment.

(Conclusion: similar bacteria, mainly skin bacteria, live on the hand and on the phone. Different kinds of bacteria, soil bacteria, live on the shoe.)

HOW TIM MET BACTEROID

Dad asked Tim not to touch anything and left the lab to run some errands. But Tim really wanted to watch some bacteria. He peeked into a microscope and saw an odd creature.

Hey you! Wipe that lens! It's me, Bacteroid! Nice to meet you!

INTERESTING FACT

Bacteroides are a special genus of bacteria. They live inside the human body and are notable for their ability to quickly adjust to any type of food. They are funny fill-bellies with a lot of flagella. And they make great friends.

24

TASK. Make the words "REDUCER" and "EXPANDER" from the letters in bubbles.

AT THE BACTERIA PARTY

At the party Tim saw many different bacteria: spherical, rodlike, short and long, spiral-like, thread-like, bean-like, with and without tails. Bacteria danced alone, in couples and in circles. Sometimes they formed a nice mishmash.

SPHERICAL BACTERIA ARE CALLED COCCI, WHICH MEANS "GRAIN" IN LATIN.

RODLIKE bacteria look like rods and they may be long short, fat or skinny, straight or twisted. Some rods are thicker in the center and some at the ends.

BACTEROID, FOR INSTANCE, IS A RODLIKE BACTERIUM.

Some rodlike bacteria have flagella to help them move around as if they were swimming. Those who don't have flagella move in a wavy motion. They aren't very fast, of course.

SPHERICAL

RODLIKE

When they reproduce, cocci make different shapes: STREPTOCOCCI line up in a row like Mom's necklace; STAPHLOCOCCI look like bunches of grapes; TETRACOCCI make a square and SARCINA — a cube; DIPLOCOCCI live in pairs and MICROCOCCI prefer being alone.

Bacteria that look like spirals, wavy lines or commas are called SPIRAL bacteria. They are spirochetes, spirilla and vibrio. Some bacteria are filamentous bacteria (look like threads), some are tetrahedral (like pyramids), some are cuboidal (like cubes), C or O-shaped, but most bacteria are spherical, rodlike or spiral.

SPIRAL

EVOLUTION

But how could teeny-tiny bacteria turn into huge dinosaurs?

Just when Tim managed to return to his normal size, Dad cam back to the lab. The working day was over and it was time t visit Mom. Tim and Dad walked outside; the warm spring su was shining.

That's a good question! The answer is evolution.

EVOLUTION (means "development" in Latin) is the natural process of wildlife development. Life on Earth began with unicellular creatures.

Those weren't the same bacteria we know today. Scientists called them archaebacteria or archaea from the Greek word meaning "ancient" or "primitive."

They developed, becoming more complex and diverse. Each new generation of microbes' descendants differed from their ancestors, acquiring new powers and even superpowers to help them reproduce. Evolution was under way.

Evolution resulted in the development of all living things on Earth, like plants, fungi, animals and people.

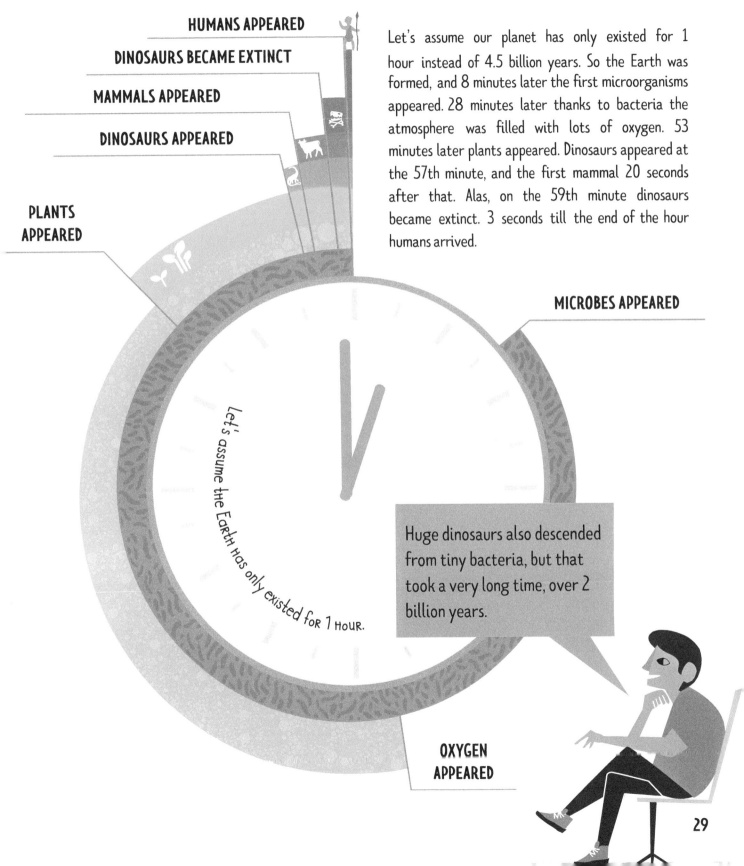

HUMANS APPEARED

DINOSAURS BECAME EXTINCT

MAMMALS APPEARED

DINOSAURS APPEARED

PLANTS APPEARED

MICROBES APPEARED

Let's assume our planet has only existed for 1 hour instead of 4.5 billion years. So the Earth was formed, and 8 minutes later the first microorganisms appeared. 28 minutes later thanks to bacteria the atmosphere was filled with lots of oxygen. 53 minutes later plants appeared. Dinosaurs appeared at the 57th minute, and the first mammal 20 seconds after that. Alas, on the 59th minute dinosaurs became extinct. 3 seconds till the end of the hour humans arrived.

Let's assume the Earth has only existed for 1 hour.

Huge dinosaurs also descended from tiny bacteria, but that took a very long time, over 2 billion years.

OXYGEN APPEARED

29

CHARLES DARWIN AND THE THEORY OF EVOLUTION

FACT!

The evolution theory was suggested and proven by a scientist called Charles Darwin.

Darwin lived in England around 200 years ago. One day he decided to circumnavigate the world aboard the ship *Beagle*. Darwin was keen on watching animals and in his travels he kept doing what he loved. On the Galapagos Islands he saw finches. On one island the finches had long thin beaks an on another – short and thick beaks like hammers. Other than that the birds were identical. Why did they have different beaks Darwin suggested that the birds who could easily find food survived and reproduced more quickly. One of the islands turned ou to have a lot of insects, making it comfortable for birds with long thin beaks who could easily reach for bugs and caterpillars.

The other island had lots of nuts, which had to be cracked, so it was more suitable for birds with hammer-like beaks. S eventually only birds with long beaks remained on one island and only birds with short beaks on the other. Darwin realized th same happened to all other animals. Those who are better adapted to their environment survive and reproduce more quickly.

This is called evolution!

30

Bacteria play an important part in evolution. Firstly, microbes change faster than any other creatures on Earth. A completely new species may appear in just 2 weeks.

Secondly, bacteria can be a tool of evolution. Scientists conducted an experiment with flies.

Bacteria which feed on starch were put into the digestive system of one group of flies. The other group of flies were given the kind which preferred malt, a substance obtained from germinated grain. Bacteria lived inside of flies and controlled their behavior.

One group was forced to eat starch and the other — malt. Soon flies with different bacteria stopped communicating with each other. They split into two species.

Quiz: "Because of evolution!"

Think of answers to the following questions:
1. Why are wolves gray, not red, blue or purple?
2. Why do elephants have long trunks and not short ones like a pig's snout?
3. Why do giraffes need long necks?

AT THE HOSPITAL

When will you get well and come back home

I don't know, honey. The doctors say I have to take antibiotics.

ANTIBIOTICS are substances that kill bacteria, both good and bad ones. "ANTI" means "against" and "BIO" means "life."

The microbes themselves use antibiotics to fight each other. Humans have learned to use their weapon and make a medicine out of it. For the first time it happened by accident.

FACT

In 1927 the scientist Sir Alexander Fleming went on vacation having left some Petri dishes with bacteria on his desk. When he got back he noticed mildew in one of the cups. It had killed the bacteria. That is how the scientist understood that mold is capable of destroying microorganisms.

Antibiotics became a sort of a magic wand for people, helping us to treat diseases caused by bacteria. It's hard to imagine now that before antibiotics people used to die from small wounds on their body or a common cold. Now antibiotics are sold in any pharmacy.

Antibiotics have their disadvantages:

- Bacteria grow resistant to antibiotics (another type of evolution). Scientists come up with new kinds of antibiotics, but bacteria learn to deal with them again.
- Antibiotics kill both the good and the bad bacteria. That weakens our health.
- Antibiotics prevent our body from recovering on its own, i.e. from forming immunity.

The doctor prescribes antibiotics if the health and life of a patient really are in danger.

You shouldn't take antibiotics unless there is no other way to recover

If you started taking antibiotics it's important to take them for as many days as prescribed by the doctor. Many patients, once they feel better, stop taking the medicine too early. Then the remaining harmful microbes both survive and develop resistance to the medicine. This leads to appearance of harmful microbes that are nearly impossible to get rid of.

Air

Tim felt sad as he was thinking of Mom. He wanted to help her, but he didn't know how. Suddenly he heard Bacteroid's voice. "You need to find good bacteria for your mom. Let's go look for them!"

There are millions of different species of bacteria on Earth. Each species has its own habitat, its own niche, as scientists put it. Some bacteria like living in rivers and seas, others in soil and even volcanic chimneys. There are also bacteria that live inside a human body.

The air is not a common habitat for bacteria. But still there are some bacteria in the air. They float on dust particles and small water drops until they settle down.

There aren't many bacteria in the air, only those that travel with the wind from one place to another. When you breathe you inhale bacteria with the air.

Some may be harmful. Luckily, you have special villi in your nose to catch bacteria.

IT'S IMPORTANT TO BLOW YOUR NOSE REGULARLY TO BREATH NORMALLY.

In the winter there are fewer microbes in the air than in the summer as the cold kills bacteria. After the rain the air is cleaner as raindrops pin bacteria down to the ground. The longer a room isn't ventilated, the more bacteria are in the air.

Will you fly with us to save my mom?

I can only live in a cloud.

Some bacteria live in the clouds. They aren't tourists who ended up in a cloud by accident, they are real sky dwellers.

There are lots of microbes in the clouds who are just waiting for a chance to get back down to Earth. By traveling through the air and the clouds bacteria spread all over the world.

Clouds are masses of water vapor. Bacteria live in small droplets like houses. They can cause rain or, the other way around, prevent regular clouds from turning into storm clouds. Bacteria may color clouds pink.

BACTERIA iN WATER

Will we find useful bacteria for Mom here?

We might. There are many different bacteria in the water.

Bacteria are the main residents of rivers, seas, lakes and oceans. Different species of bacteria live in water bodies, some are at the surface, and some are deep down. Even water from different shores of a lake may contain different bacteria.

Bacteria purify water by eating dead fish, insects and plants. Many clams, worms and other animals eat bacteria, they are their basic diet. Some larger inhabitants of rivers and seas also eat bacteria without even noticing. A whale, for example, eats up billions of billions of bacteria as it swallows plankton.

There exist bioluminescent bacteria that are kind of like biological light bulbs and can light up. Many water dwellers give shelter to luminescent bacteria and use them as camouflage to hide from predators, or the other way around, to hunt their prey.

INTERESTING FACT

The deep water angler fish has a rod on its head, the end of which is populated with luminescent bacteria. They light up when the angler needs them to. The angler uses their light to attract small fish it feeds on.

A relationship in which living things cohabit and help each other is called a SYMBIOSIS.

But bacteria are small, and the raindrop still has enough room for them to swim around.

Water is home to cyanobacteria, the ancestors of all plants of Earth. Just like plants, they feed on sunlight and are green.

When they reproduce, cyanobacteria line up in long chains that look like thin green threads. You can see cyanobacteria on underwater rocks or floating in water.

By the way, the color of water largely depends on bacteria. They can give water different tints. Just think about it, bacteria are artists.

Cyanobacteria and luminescent bacteria have superpowers! But they aren't any good to treat Mom.

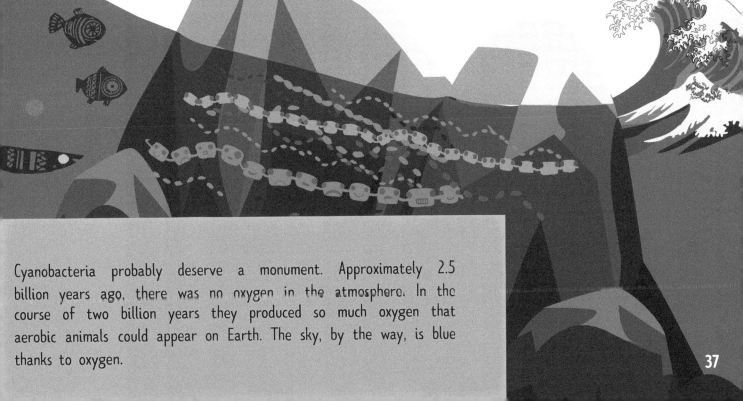

Cyanobacteria probably deserve a monument. Approximately 2.5 billion years ago, there was no oxygen in the atmosphere. In the course of two billion years they produced so much oxygen that aerobic animals could appear on Earth. The sky, by the way, is blue thanks to oxygen.

SOiL

SOIL is a thin layer of the Earth's surface which nourishes plants and gives life to underground animals, worms and insects. To tell you the truth, soil gives life to everyone: without it there wouldn't be plants, which means no insects, no animals and no us. Soil is a mixture of organic and non-organic substances.

NON-ORGANIC SUBSTANCES are everything that is produced without wildlife: rocks, water and salt. **ORGANIC SUBSTANCES** are mainly produced by living organisms: bacteria, plants and animals. Once upon a time our planet didn't have any soil, only lifeless rocks which couldn't grow a single blade of grass. Some bacteria adjusted to living on bare rocks. They fed on sunlight, taking some nutrients from the air and some from rock. These bacteria excreted acid, which eroded the rock giving bacteria more food.

  Following these bacteria the rocks were populated by lichen, then ferns and other plants, shrubs and trees. Plants died and turned into humus, which mixed with chunks of rock and became more nutrients for new plants. This is how a layer of fertile soil appeared. And we have bacteria to thank for that, which still play an important part in maintaining the composition of soil.

Most modern bacteria which live in soil do a very important job: they feed on dead animals and plants, turning organic substances into non-organic ones: salt, water and gas. Will you come with me and help my mom?

There are many fascinating bacteria in soil. Like RHIZOBIA, for example.

These bacteria live in the roots of plants, forming small tubers (spheres). The plant feeds rhizobia with sugar, excreting it from its roots, and in turn rhizobia provide a substance the plants need for growth.

Help Tim get to the Bacteroid!

Are you going to help my mom?

We are well fed here!

THE NATURAL CYCLE OF MATTER

Soil appeared on our planet thanks to the cycle of matter.
Non-organic substances turn into organic ones and back.

The interchange of matter is continuous, and life on our planet depends on it.
The word "CYCLE" means movement in a circle.

The change of seasons — spring, summer, autumn, winter and back to spring — is a cycle.

There are a number of natural cycles. The most important one is the GEOLOGICAL CYCLE — these are changes happening deep underground, where a hot melted substance called lava lurks. Lava is always in motion and it sets continents and seas in motion as well, but they move so slowly that we never notice.

Another important cycle is the WATER CYCLE.

You can watch it when it's raining or snowing. Water gets onto soil and drains deep underground, into subterranean rivers that flow into ordinary water bodies, like seas and oceans.

Then water evaporates from the surface of rivers, lakes, seas, oceans as well as the ground, the trees and the grass. Water vapor rises up and forms clouds; regular clouds turn into rain clouds and the water falls down again in the form of rain only to evaporate again later.

By following this path again and again water gives life to all living things.

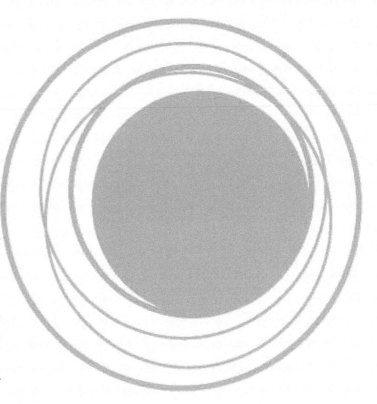

THE BIOLOGICAL CYCLE

But the most interesting cycle is the **BIOLOGICAL** one. It's very complicated. And all of us are part of it.

> **BIOLOGICAL CYCLE** is continuous transformation of substances from non-organic to organic and back.

The foundation of the biological cycle is sunlight. Plants absorb the sun's energy, water and minerals from soil and turn them into organic substances: leaves, grass, tree branches and trunks. They transform non-organic substances to organic.

Plants are eaten by herbivorous animals and give them energy for growth. Herbivorous animals are eaten by predators. Humans eat both plants and animals. Animals, birds and humans eat organic matter, but do not transform it into non-organic matter.

This is where bacteria come into play. They eat dead animals and plants and everything organic and turn it into mineral substances: gas, water, salts and metals.

In the BIOLOGICAL CYCLE living organisms process substances making them suitable for use by others. Microbes play the most important part in this cycle. Without animals and even plants the biological cycle, however slow, would go on. But without bacteria and other microorganisms it will stop, as will life on Earth.

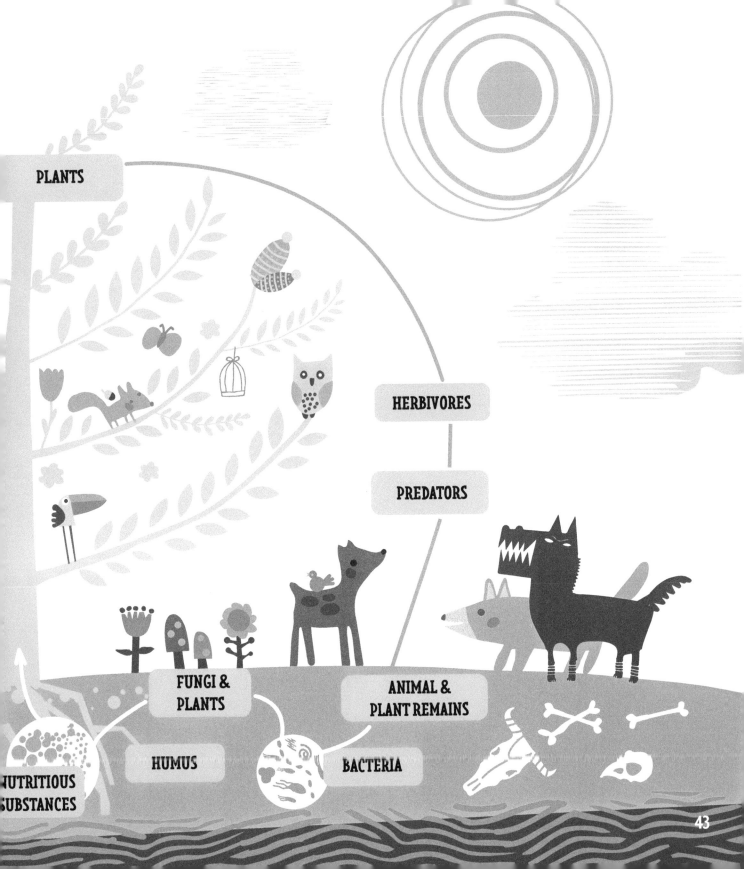

PLANTS

HERBIVORES

PREDATORS

FUNGI &
PLANTS

ANIMAL &
PLANT REMAINS

NUTRITIOUS
SUBSTANCES

HUMUS

BACTERIA

43

EXTREMOPHiLES

Despite the fact that bacteria are protozoa they are not as primitive as they may seem. There are bacteria which inhabit places where no other living being can survive.

Bacteria that like extreme environments are called **EXTREMOPHILES.**

When we boil water, bacteria in it die. But there are bacteria which easily live in fountains of boiling water coming from underground. These fountains — hot springs — are the favorite habitat for hyperthermophiles. In winter, when the weather is frosty, most bacteria die.

EXTREME ENVIRONMENTS are those where it's extremely cold or extremely hot, with no air or with dangerous radiation. For example, in outer space the conditions are extreme and in order to survive there astronauts do not only need a space suit, but also strong health and long training. But there are bacteria which easily live in space without any training or spacesuits.

But not all of them! Bacteria called Planococcus halocryophilus love negative temperatures. They live far north in the Arctic.

Bacteria called Deinococcus radiodurans are considered the toughest bacteria in the world. It's not because they are mean. It's just that these superabcteria can survive in the icy outer space, in acid, or in vacuum and are resistant to radiation.

Even Superman wouldn't survive in such environments. But Deinococcus radiodurans feels great.

Superbacteria! They are exactly what we need! They will be able to help mom!

They might be, but where shall we find them? We cannot hop on a feather and fly into space.

45

BACTERIA RULE THE WORLD

Microbes do not only live in the environment around us. They also live inside of animals. To be honest, animals, fish and insects wouldn't be able to live without them. And humans, too. Scientists have found bacteria inside humans and most living creatures. They are found in mosquitoes, sea clams, worms, gorillas and turtles. What are they doing there? They are helping us.

An Euprymna squid looks like a little cute octopus, but unlike one it is covered with pretty luminescent spots. The squid is born without these spots. But after a while its body is inhabited by bacteria thanks to which the squid starts gleaming.

Half of a Paracatenula flatworm consists of bacteria. In fact it's just a long sack with a brain on one of the ends. The worm lives on the ocean floor and feeds on sulfur, or rather the bacteria inside of it feed on sulfur, and it feeds on their leftovers. If we split this worm in two, each new part will grow a new head. This worm has the power to grow new body parts thanks to bacteria.

Laughing hyenas use bacteria to tell their relatives about themselves: whether they are a boy or a girl, how old and how healthy they are, who their family are and where they live. A hyena can share this information via the scent it leaves on the grass. And the scent is controlled by bacteria living on its body.

By the way, the same applies to people, although we aren't very good scent experts. Nevertheless we can tell that every person smells in their own way. This scent is defined by bacteria living on a person's skin. It's the bacteria that produce this scent. If the same bacteria live on your skin and on your mom's skin, your scents will be similar and you are likely to think that your mom smells nice. But it wasn't you who decided so, it was your bacteria! They influence the way we perceive smells.

Perhaps it's your bacteria and not you that chooses who to make friends with, when to go play outside and what to eat. That's right, they are sitting inside of you, looking into a periscope and controlling you like a robot. Scared? Just kidding! You aren't a robot, and bacteria don't have a periscope. But they do influence you, even though you might not notice it.

Why are bacteria so important for our body?

Remember that humans have just recently appeared in the world, where microbes have lived for billions of years. They had ruled our planet long before the first animals appeared.

BACTERIA INSIDE A HUMAN BODY

If we examine our skin under a microscope, we will see small peas, fat rods and tailed beans. These are skin bacteria.

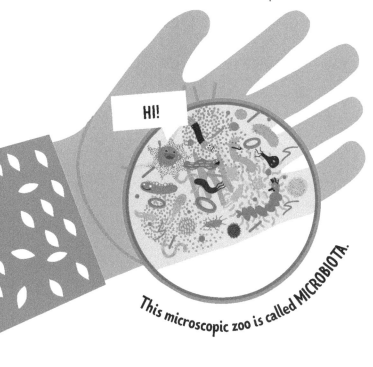

HI!

This microscopic zoo is called MICROBIOTA.

These small creatures also live inside of us. Even when you are alone, you aren't alone. Your microbe friends are with you.

For every cell of the human body there is one bacterium, so you can't really tell who lives on who.

When babies are born, there are no bacteria on their body. Little by little microscopic inhabitants populate them like a planet. Mainly the baby gets the microbes from his or her mom. But clearly they get new species of bacteria from Dad, other family members, pets and the world around them. As the baby grows their microbiota changes, it becomes more diverse, more complex and more interesting.

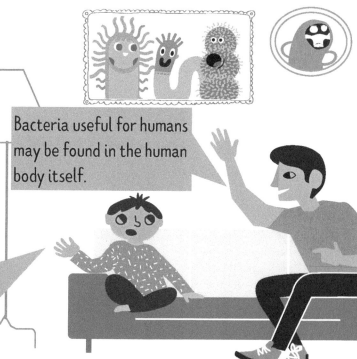

Bacteria useful for humans may be found in the human body itself.

Where can we get useful bacteria for Mom? I've looked everywhere, both in water and soil.

What good do microbes do inside of us?

Firstly, they help to digest food we aren't capable of digesting ourselves. Without bacteria, vegetables and leafy greens would only be half-digested. And, valuable substances yielded from dietary fibers wouldn't bring us any good. Strawberries, raspberries, grapes and even oats we eat are finished by our bacteria.

Bacteria produce some vitamins and essential substances we don't get with food.

Bacteria deal with poisonous substances that get inside us by accident, for example, with spoiled food.

They protect us from bad bacteria, prevent them from settling inside us or kill them. They teach our immunity to tell apart good and harmful bacteria and to destroy only the bad guys.

They influence the way we perceive smells and even our mood.

There is a **SYMBIOSIS** between a human being and its bacteria. That means we have made a pact to help each other. We become a home for our bacteria and feed them. They return the favor by doing us good.

In order to increase the number of good bacteria inside, a person may take PROBIOTICS and PREBIOTICS.

PROBIOTICS are good bacteria put into a capsule by scientists, so that a person could swallow them and let them settle inside.

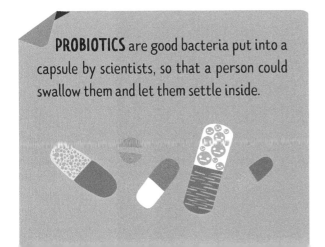

PREBIOTICS are food for the good bacteria. People take them so that the good bacteria have enough food.

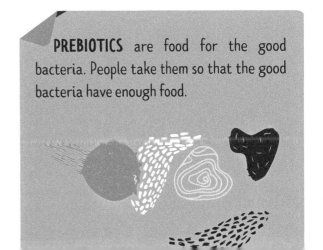

A JOURNEY INSIDE

Tim and Bacteroid decided to search for good bacteria inside Dad. Every day Tim's dad has been taking prebiotics — tablets that look like capsules of a spaceship. Tim and Bacteroid climbed into one of those capsules. Unsuspecting, Tim's dad swallowed the capsule and our friends set out on an exciting journey inside the human body.

The human mouth is a real miniature zoo. Most bacteria are permanent residents of this area. The environment inside your mouth is similar to that of a seaside resort — it's warm, humid and there's plenty of food. That's why the bacteria here are highly diverse.

Spheres, rods, something like corn ears and spherical brushes, snakes, spirals, tailed commas — there are over 500 species of bacteria in your mouth. Some stick to one spot, others float in the saliva by moving their flagella.

There are villain microbes in your mouth too, who only pretend to be good while our immunity is strong.

The main enemy of our teeth is called **STREPTOCOCCUS MUTANS.** It's a tricky microbe with a soft spot for sugar. It is the one that damages our teeth. That's why grownups often tell kids that sugar is bad for their teeth. That's true.

But you have to keep an eye on the bacteria in your mouth. To make sure your teeth are healthy never let bacteria settle on them. That's why you have to brush your teeth twice a day in the morning and in the evening.

Tooth enamel is designed in way that makes it difficult for bacteria to stick to it. But some manage to succeed and teeth get covered with plaque, which attracts even more bacteria.
DENTAL PLAQUE is colonies of microbes, which damage your teeth.

Saliva contains MUCIN, a substance that covers your teeth with a special film to protect them from bacteria.

Thanks to mucin you can blow bubbles with your saliva.

At night salivary glands sleep just like we do, so bacteria throw a party inside your mouth: when left unsupervised they settle anywhere they want, eat whatever they want and reproduce uncontrollably. That's why we sometimes get morning breath.

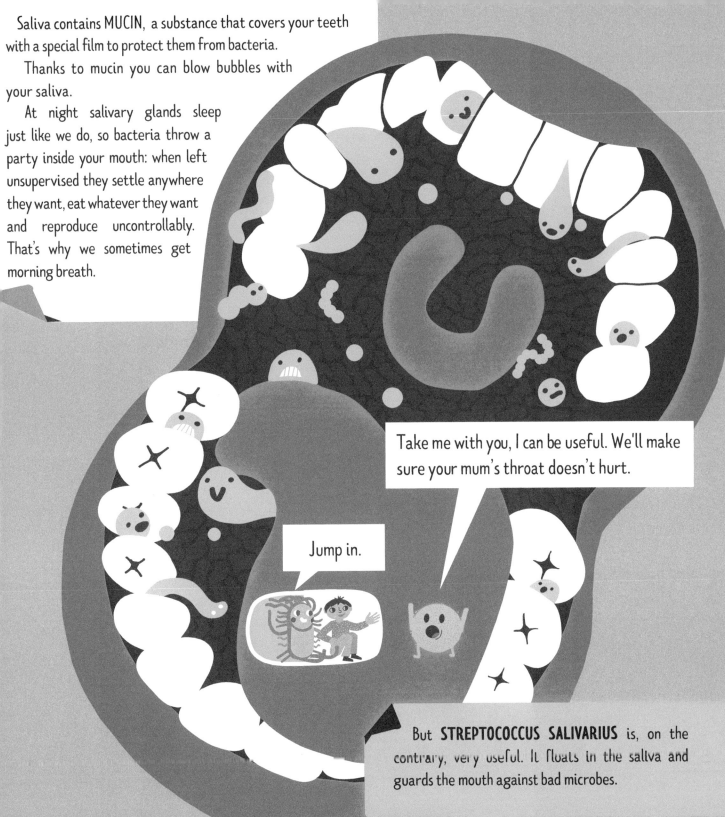

Take me with you, I can be useful. We'll make sure your mum's throat doesn't hurt.

Jump in.

But **STREPTOCOCCUS SALIVARIUS** is, on the contrary, very useful. It floats in the saliva and guards the mouth against bad microbes.

IN THE THROAT

The travelers' capsule was sailing through a cave. Further ahead a stalactite hung down from a moist pink cave roof. The cave's floor was covered with a carpet of moving villi, among which something like mushroom caps stuck out here and there. The capsule floated over the tongue and headed to the throat.

The villi of the carpet and the mushroom cap bumps are our tongue's taste buds. With their help we can taste the food and tell whether it's sweet, salty, sour or bitter. When you chew up your food it gets mixed with saliva and hits the surface of a taste bud. The taste bud tries it, and sends the information to your brain. Since taste buds retain food particles on the tongue, it's a paradise for bacteria. The plaque on your tongue has to be cleaned just like the plaque on your teeth. Especially before you go to sleep, so that there aren't too many bacteria. You can use a toothbrush or a special scraper to clean your tongue.

This is us! We are looking for good bacteria for Mom!

Deep inside your mouth the landscape is completely different: there are many round pink bumps crawling on top of each other. These are tonsils — security posts guarding our body against harmful microbes. Tonsils are home to guards called immune cells, which do everything not to let microbes in. We have tonsils on the tongue, called lingual tonsils, and at the sides of the throat, called palatine tonsils.

Sometimes tonsils make mistakes and take good bacteria hostage. Or put too many bacteria in jail. Then tonsils begin to inflame and may be removed by a doctor. It's not a big deal; the throat still has other watch posts.

Halt! Who goes there?

You must have had a sore throat before. It happened because bad microbes were caught in the throat and your immunity fought them. Since bacteria reproduce quickly, the best way to help your immunity when you are ill is to rinse your throat with medicine to wash away the bad bacteria.

ESOPHAGUS

The **ESOPHAGUS** is a smooth, narrow tube to transport the chewed up food to the stomach.

Take a bite of something, an apple, for example. Chew it well and swallow. Now count to eight. One, two, three... When you get to eight, the food will have traveled through the esophagus to your stomach.

Water and other liquids you drink slip through in just two seconds.

When our travelers approached the strange pink bump hanging down like a stalactite, the cave shuddered and closed. Dad had swallowed the capsule. So the friends rushed down the narrow tunnel, like a high slide in a water park. The food does not just fall down. If it were so, astronauts in space would not be able to eat. That's because there's weightlessness in space and nothing ever falls down. The food moves along the esophagus to the stomach, because there is a force that pushes it through. It's called peristalsis.

Your esophagus is made of muscle. Just like the muscles of your arms it can contract and relax. Your esophagus is designed in a way that it relaxes when it lets food through. Then it contracts and pushes it forward. Can you imagine? You don't even have to think about it! The esophagus muscles work on their own. I wish it worked the same way with pull-ups.

There are two doors in the esophagus which let visitors through only one way. These doors are called valves or esophageal sphincters. One of them is located at the top, right after the throat. The second one is at the bottom, close to the stomach. When food approaches, the door opens to let the train through and then closes.

If it weren't for these valves, each time we turned upside down or laughed food would come back out of us. That would sure be inconvenient.

The esophagus is home to some bacteria, but they are just a very few small spherical Streptococci. They end up in the esophagus with the food and slip down with it. It's hard to live in a tunnel where trains loaded with food rush through at high speeds.

This is the eso-o-ophagus.

Wow, cool!

Help! Save us!

55

STOMACH

The capsule with our friends slipped out of the esophagus and entered a large boiling lake in the stomach. Your stomach is a sac where food is digested. When we eat, the stomach stretches out and kneads the food inside, excreting stomach juice. This juic is very sour. It helps us to dissolve food into the smallest particles called molecules.

The environment in the stomach is extremely adverse. Bacteria cannot live here.

The stomach protects us from harmful microbes, which could have slipped through with the food. In order to protect itself from the acid it produces, the insides of the stomach are covered with protective mucus. Due to this fact the stomach is populated with only one species of bacteria capable of surviving in such a hostile environment. It is called Helicobacter pylori.

Don't worry! We'll make it!

Watch out! The capsule is melting! We'll all die!

Please, go ahead.

Faster! We have to hurry.

At the exit to the stomach there is a valve called the gatekeeper. A gatekeeper is actually a person who opens and closes gates. In the stomach this valve lets through digested food: not all of it at once, but in small portions, just right for the intestines that come immediately after the stomach to process it. It's a very smart valve.

Helicobacter pylori is a green rod with flagella at the ends. It uses the flagella to hide in the mucus on the stomach walls and quickly swims in the stomach juice. Helicobacter pylori can also envelope itself in liquid to protect it against the acidic stomach juice. This bacterium's life is hard. It always has to hide to stay away from corrosive acid. No wonder it has such a bad attitude. Sometimes it gets angry and can start nibbling on the stomach walls, causing such diseases as gastritis and gastric ulcer.

When scientists discovered that gastritis is caused by bacteria, they started treating patients with antibiotics. Helicobacter pylori lives in many people's stomachs. Tim's dad also has it. In most people it doesn't cause the disease. But if a person is often stressed and angry, their stomach starts working badly and then Helicobacter pylori can show its ill nature.

It's better not to make it angry.

BIOLOGICAL HAZARD

INTERESTING FACT

Heliobacter pylori was discovered in 1979 by scientists Barry Marshall and Robin Warren. They proved that these bacteria can cause stomach disease in humans, called gastritis. They were given a Nobel Prize, the most prestigious award in the world.

DUODENUM

As soon as the food leaves the stomach it enters the duodenum.

The life of microbes in the duodenum is not easy. On top of the fact that food comes from the stomach mixed with acidic stomach juice, it also gets some bile from the gallbladder which is extremely bitter, but is required for digestion of fat. Some bacteria live here as well. Small villages of bacteria have settled on the walls of the duodenum.

The main street in the Firmicute village is called the Enterococci Street, and a whole Enterococci family lives there.

The most interesting part about the duodenum (short for "intestinum duodenum digitorum") is its name. In ancient Latin it means "the intestine of twelve finger-widths."

"Digitorum" means finger. And "duodenum digitorium" means twelve fingers. So someone used their finger to measure the length of this intestine section. You must be wondering how they did that.

ENTEROCOCCI are oval or spherical bacteria who live in pairs or in short chains. Enterococci is a common family name. Among them there are criminals and hooligans, who cause diseases. But mainly Enterococci are peaceful bacteria, which inhabit the mucous membrane of the intestines and protect their settlements from attacks of bad microbes.

INTERESTING FACT

The main job of the duodenum is to turn the acidic mash coming from the stomach into something suitable for the intestines. For that the duodenum excretes enzymes which mix up with the food and neutralize the acid.

FIRMICUTES

Other residents of the duodenum are ACTINO-BACTERIA or ACTINOMYCETES. They are resistant to acidic environments, and not scared of the stomach juice at all. Actinomycetes are long thin rods that look like threads. By the way, a multitude of their relatives live in soil.

Some species have settled in the human intestines. Perhaps primitive people didn't wash their vegetables before eating, so actinomycetes settled down inside.

Actinomycetes are very militant when attacked by other bacteria and may excrete an antibiotic to kill their enemies. People have learned to use the antibiotic produced by actinomycetes to treat infections.

Bacteria are classified into phyla, classes, orders, families, genera and species. It's hard to tell who is related to whom. Scientists have to read the DNA, the genetic information inside the bacteria, to tell them apart.

ACTINOMYCETES

Come with us.
You know your way around here.

59

THE DIGESTION FACTORY:
SMALL INTESTINE

After the duodenum the travelers found themselves in the small intestine. It's a long thin tube folded in loops inside your belly.

The intestine varies in width along its length. On average it's 2 to 3 cm wide (about 1 inch).

But if you unfold the small intestine, its length will reach 3 meters. Or even 7 meters when it's relaxed. That's 23 feet long! But it is never relaxed; it even works at night.

THE WAVELIKE MOTIONS OF THE INTESTINES THAT PUSH FORWARD THEIR CONTENTS ARE CALLED PERISTALSIS.

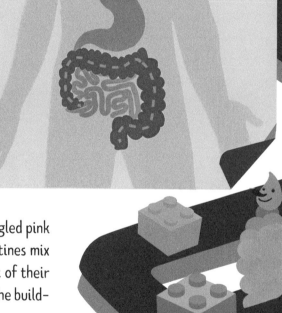

If we could look at our intestines from the outside, we would see a tangled pink tube, which is constantly moving, contracting and relaxing. The intestines mix up and digest food, pushing it further along. The most important part of their job is absorption of nutrients obtained from digested food. Those are the building blocks — molecules of proteins, carbs and fats.

INTERESTING FACT

All food in all its shapes and sizes mainly consists of proteins, fats and carbohydrates. Proteins are the building blocks for our body. Carbs are the source of energy.

Fats store the energy. Also, we need fats for digestion of some vitamins and proper functioning of our brain.

Food moves along the intestines, chewed up and mixed with saliva, stomach juice and enzymes.

The stomach juice (not to be confused with apple juice) and enzymes (special substances needed for digestion) are excreted in the stomach and the intestines after you have eaten.

BILE

ENZYMES

STOMACH JUICE

You might think: Ew! Yucky! But in fact, the streamlined work of the digestion factory is a miracle created by nature. Thanks to this factory everything we eat decomposes into small blocks — molecules used by our body to build itself.

61

DAD HAS HAD LUNCH

Our travelers hadn't' gone far when they heard a strange humming sound behind them. Something was quickly approaching them along the dark corridor. Suddenly the flow picked them up and carried them along the intestines. Luckily, Bacteroid managed to grab a villus. He helped everyone to dry land. An endless forest of pink trees unfolded before the travelers.

What was that?

Dad has had lunch.

Hold on to Bacteroid!

Help! We are going to die!

There are a little more bacteria in the small intestine than in the duodenum. Here they live in small towns, not villages. Rods, long sprawling threads and necklaces of spherical bacteria, cover the inner walls of the small intestine and stretch like garlands from one wall to another. All these small creatures are constantly swarming, busy with their microbe lives, and try not to intervene in the work of the small intestine, the job of which is to absorb as many nutrients from food as possible.

From the inside the intestines consist of hills and folds. They are covered with villi on which smaller villi and microvilli grow. For bacteria it's a hilly area covered in trees.

Each villus is like a pump with a conveyor: it absorbs molecules of nutrients and passes them further along. The openings between microvilli are small. Bacteria do not fit through.

Inside each villus there is a blood vessel — a thin tube for blood to run through. Nutrients get into blood and move further into the body like ships along a river. Blood transports nutrients, energy and building blocks to where they are needed.

We digest most food ourselves. Bacteria get whatever we failed to digest.

INTESTINAL IMMUNITY

The intestines are protected by immune cells which are always on guard. They hide behind the absorptive villi and cover the whole inner surface of the intestines. Immune cells personally know all good bacteria living in the intestines and meet all newcomers, to decide whether they can stay or have to be banished from the body.

The immunity always has to restrain itself not to kill useful bacteria. The older a person is the more their immunity knows about bacteria and the wiser it behaves.

Unfortunately, with age the immunity wears out. To make sure it doesn't happen, you should lead a healthy life: eat healthily, get enough sleep and exercise.

To maintain order in the intestines and to guard it against unwanted bacteria our body built a great wall of mucus. A double thick layer of mucus covers the intestine walls from the inside and prevents bacteria from penetrating deeper.

Deep inside the mucus there live bacteriophages — viruses preying on bacteria. Viruses are very odd creatures which can barely be called creatures. They are DNA with legs. If a bacterium manages to overcome the mucus wall and bacteriophages and penetrate into the intestine wall, it will be retained by brave border guards — the immune cells. They will escort good bacteria back to where they belong and destroy the bad ones.

Bacteriophage viruses can be found anywhere, but in the intestinal mucosa they are particularly numerous. If a bacterium slips deeper inside, bacteriophages will destroy it. Here's how it happens: a bacteriophage grabs the bacterium with its legs, pokes a small hole in its shell and injects its own DNA, information foreign to the microbe. The bacterium then goes crazy and starts reproducing a virus inside itself until it finally explodes. It's kind of a delayed action bomb.

Will you come with us to save my mom?

Yes! Count me in!

The small intestine is home to long threadlike bacteria which belong to the class of Clostridia. They are called threadlike or filamentous (from the English word "filament" meaning "thread"). They are real bullies. Their job is to tease the immunity so that it stays alert. Thanks to Clostridia the small intestine doesn't have many bacteria which could prevent it from absorbing nutrients from food.

THE APPENDIX IS A DEAD END

APPENDIX

The APPENDIX is a small dead-ended tube in the intestine labyrinth, which leads nowhere. If you look at it from the outside, it looks like a tail the size of your middle finger.

The sign says APPENDIX.

Where are we?

A-a-a-ah! We are lost.

Let me check the

Our travelers wandered along the long corridor of the small intestine for a long time. Sometimes they had to climb up, sometimes they slid down the slippery wrinkled surface, past villi and small bacterial settlements. Finally they approached an opening at the end of the corridor. The arches of the opening suddenly contracted, swallowing the travelers and they fell into the darkness.

We have to move by touch.

The word appendix came to English from Latin. The appendix is not involved in the digestion of food. It's a miniature lab in the intestines, where immune cells study microbes. Good bacteria are allowed to stay in the appendix. When the intestines are upset and all bacteria are evacuated, or when they are destroyed by antibiotics, good bacteria will populate the intestines again and restore their proper functioning.

Restoration of microbiota after an illness is the appendix's main job.

Sometimes bad bacteria get inside the appendix and that may cause an inflammation called appendicitis. If doctors cannot treat the inflammation, they remove the appendix.

People whose appendix have been removed and anyone who has undergone treatment with antibiotics or has suffered an intestinal upset are strongly recommended to take probiotics and prebiotics to restore life on Mars... Just kidding. To restore proper microbiota in the intestines.

People whose appendix has been removed live just like anyone else. The job of training the immunity and studying bacteria is taken over by the immune cells of the intestines, although it's not as convenient as a special lab is.

LARGE INTESTINES, BACTERIA METROPOLISES

We are in New York City!

Or maybe London!

Amazing!

We are in the large intestine.

If a person is a planet for bacteria, then the large intestine is its most densely populated continent. The large intestine is home to more species of bacteria than there are species of animals on Earth!

Why do you think it's called large? Is it because it makes people larger?

Not at all! It is large compared to the small intestine. That is due to the fact that the work of the large intestine requires more room. The large intestine, just like the small one, is always in motion as it pushes its contents towards the exit.

THE WIDTH OF THE LARGE INTESTINE IS 6 TO 7 CM (2.5 IN) AND ITS LENGTH IS 150 CM (59 IN).

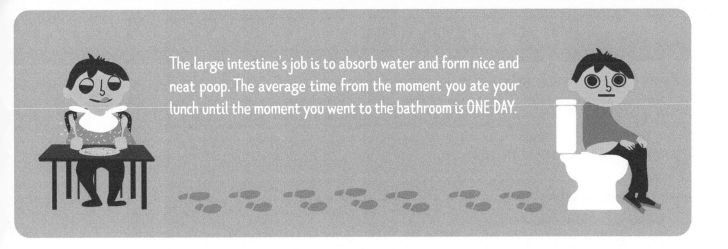

The large intestine's job is to absorb water and form nice and neat poop. The average time from the moment you ate your lunch until the moment you went to the bathroom is ONE DAY.

The large intestine absorbs liquid from the food (or rather from what's left of it). If it weren't for its work, we would have to drink an extra 2 to 4 liters (.5 to 1 gallon) of water every day. It is in the large intestine where most bacteria live. The majority of its residents have grown so used to their habitat that should they find themselves somewhere else they would die. Bacteria live in the intestines like people in cities: they go to work and perform many different tasks for the good of the microbe community and the human body. Although, to be honest, bacteria don't have to go anywhere. Many of them can't even move. They can perform their primary tasks without leaving their places.

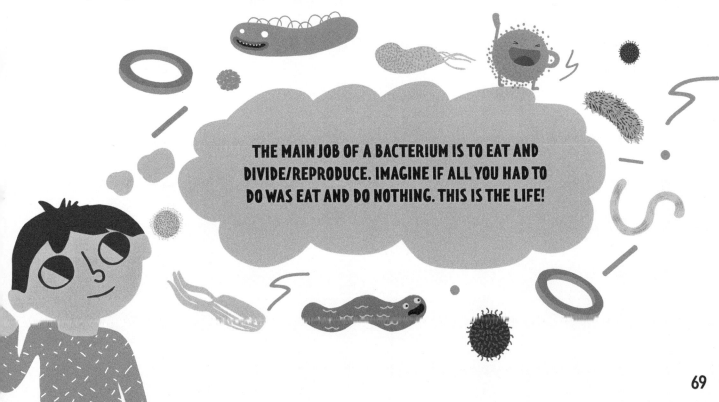

THE MAIN JOB OF A BACTERIUM IS TO EAT AND DIVIDE/REPRODUCE. IMAGINE IF ALL YOU HAD TO DO WAS EAT AND DO NOTHING. THIS IS THE LIFE!

HEALTHY FOOD

Without bacteria, the nutrients from fiber would go to waste. And we would be left without extra energy, vitamins B and K, as well as without help to our immunity and protection of our intestines from hostile troops.

As you must have already figured out, we feed our bacteria with whatever we eat. Their food consists of undigested leftovers of our food and a little bit of mucus produced by the intestines.

If you eat an apple, only pieces of its skin and undigested fibers will make it to the large intestine. They are eaten by bacteria.

Our body cannot digest fiber. It's very hard and consists of long complex molecules. But bacteria can. That's why they are useful. Fiber contains the elements we need.

I am hungry, by the way!

INTERESTING FACT

FIBER is the hard shells of a plant cell and sugar polymers. Fiber molecules are found in plant foods, like cereals, nuts, fruit, vegetables and so on.

In order not to deprive the good bacteria of their breakfast, lunch and dinner we have to eat food that is rich in fiber.

When bacteria inside of us feel good, we feel great. Healthy eating may be visualised as a dinner plate.

HEALTHY EATING PLATE

Eat a lot of fruits and vegetables, at least 5 portions a day. One portion is the size of your palm.

Grains, potatoes, bread, rice and pasta are great base foods. Choose whole-grain options.

Beans, fish, meat and eggs are sources of protein, the building material for our body.

Milk, cheese, and yogurt are sources of protein and calcium for the bones.

Sweets, chips and soft drinks are not needed for your body. You can eat them on special occasions like holidays.

Liquid is very important for your body, you can choose tea or juice, but CLEAN WATER is the best.

Plant oils are beneficial in small amounts.

UNHEALTHY FOOD

What happens when we eat food that lacks dietary fiber?

Sugar, ice-cream, candy and white bread are simple carbohydrates which don't contain fiber and are immediately digested.

Molecules of simple carbohydrates are decomposed into blocks as early as the stomach and the small intestine. This way hardly anything reaches the bacteria in the large intestine. Many bacteria starve to death.

Excess of fast carbohydrates, especially sugar, at the expense of fibers is not only harmful, because it makes our bacteria starve, it is also bad for our metabolism.

But why are they so tasty?

Sugar quickly gives us energy, that's why simple carbohydrates are also called fast. You don't have to wait until food goes the whole way from the stomach to the large intestine. Our body loves energy, even if there's too much of it. And the taste buds on our tongue are designed in a way that makes them like sweet things.

METABOLISM is a magic process of transformation of one substance into another, which takes place inside the human body and the body of any other living being to keep it alive.

People didn't use to eat a lot of sugar. 200 years ago only noblemen and rich people could afford sugar or sweets. Today sugar is produced on an industrial scale, added to yogurt, drinks, sauces, cereals and even ham, not to mention candy, ice-cream, cakes and other sweets.

Food producers know that people like sugar, so they add it to everything to sell more products.

How much sugar does a person eat in a year?

200 years ago – 2 kilos (4.4 lbs)
Today – 37 kilos (81.5lbs)

Another harmful substance found in food is **PRESERVATIVES.** They are added to food to prevent it from spoiling, i.e. to keep bacteria away. It's amazing that a cupcake can stay fresh for up to several months, because bacteria don't eat it. The only problem is that such a cupcake could hurt our intestinal bacteria.

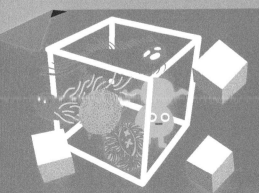

When our body gets too much energy, it cannot spend it all and stores it in the form of fat. After eating something sweet we soon feel hungry and tired again. Consumption of large amounts of sugar leads to obesity and may cause different diseases, like diabetes.

INTESTINAL MAFIA

Tell the brain we want more sugar! And hurry up!

Got sugar? What if I find some?

What are these?

They are mafia!

Oh dear! Hooligans!

There are bacteria who love sweets as much as kids do. Sugar is usually digested in the stomach and absorbed in the small intestine. But if a person eats a lot of sugar, some of it might reach the large intestine.

Bacteria with a sweet tooth rush to the sweet food and quickly shovel it up. If your diet only has sugar and starch and lacks healthy fiber-containing products like cereal, legumes, fruit and vegetables, regular hard-working bacteria like rods and long threads are left without food and starve to death. Entire settlements and towns die out. The bacteria community become less diverse.

It doesn't mean bacteria have a sweet tooth. They just like sugar. They eat it up quickly, since very little of it every reaches the intestines where they live. Besides, sugar molecules are simple and there's no need to gnaw on them or solve them with enzymes for a long time, as it happens with complex carbohydrates.

We are big and a grain of sugar seems small to us. But for bacteria it's the size of a huge house!

Modern research suggests that our mood depends on the intestines as they send many signals to the brain.

Microbes have learned to produce signal substances called **NEUROTRANSMITTERS** which they use to send their messages to the brain.

What a delicious cake!

You don't like broccoli and only crave sweet buns? That is because the sweet tooth bacteria mafia signals your brain that they want sugar.

The intestines and the brain exchange signals with the help of the vagus nerve which connects these two organs like a telephone cable.

THE VAGUS NERVE is a long pair of nerves stretching from the brain to all internal organs.

AT THE FESTIVAL

There are thousands of different species of bacteria in the intestines, many of which are relatives, close and distant ones. Among intestine microbes there are four communities which are the most numerous.

The BACTEROIDETES phylum (a huge family) is one of the most influential in the large intestine. Chubby rods with many flagella, they like complex sugars, like those contained in fruit and fiber.

Bacteroidetes are good at guarding the intestines from bad microbes.

The FIRMICUTES phylum unifies many families. Bacteria of this group may look like spheres, rods, have flagella or no flagella, look like beans or spindles.

Firmucutes have two major classes: Bacilli and Clostridia.

Their classes are not the same as classes in school. In biology, classes are formed based on properties and peculiarities. As if at school there were classes for redheads or excellent students only.

The most useful bacilla are LACTOBACILLI. Lactobacteria or lactobacilli are the first to populate our intestines and we get them from our moms. Breast milk feeds them since they like lactose — a carbohydrate contained in dairy products. They turn it into lactic acid which kills harmful bacteria.

The group of PROTEOBACTERIA includes many species of many different shapes and properties: spherical, rodlike, spiral. The scary Helicobacter pylori is, perhaps, the most well-known intestinal bacterium. The Escherichia coli is, by the way, also one of proteobacteria.

LACTOBACILLA

INTERESTING FACT

The Escherichia coli owes its popularity to the fact that it was the first intestinal bacteria to be discovered. Scientist Theodor Escherich found and described it in 1885, more than 130 years ago. Since then, scientists managed to study it well mainly thanks to the fact that it reproduces well in a Petri dish.

It seems we have walked into a party!

Yes! Here are my relatives!

INTERESTING FACT

Microbiologist Carl Woese studied bacteria and discovered a similarity between some species. It happened in 1987. He classified them under the name proteobacteria. Dr. Woese himself referred to them as purple bacteria and their relatives. Indeed, most proteobacteria are purple.

And mine! And mine!

ACTINOBACTERIA are a very large gut microbial community. We have met their representatives before. There are a lot of actinobacteria inside the human body. But there are also plenty of them in the environment: in soil, on plants and even on the walls of our apartments.

ACTINOBACTERIA

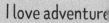

BIFIDOBACTERIA

The most important species of bacteria useful for the human body are BIFIDOBACTERIA — they are short rods sometimes with bulbs at the ends that look like tree branches.

Wait up, I'm coming with you!

I love adventure[s]

Bifidobacteria provide us with B vitamins, as well as the vitamin K and useful acids which protect the intestinal walls. You can buy Bifidobacteria in capsules in a pharmacy.

Apart from these major groups there are other microorganisms. Like ARCHAEA, for example, which eat up leftovers other bacteria didn't finish. We can also find YEAST in the intestines. Those are small budding ellipsoids.

Then there are the shapeless **TENERICUTES,** which are considered tiny even in the bacteria universe. Tenericutes don't have a cell wall which gives bacteria their shape. They only have the soft membrane which flexes in response to any push.

Small families of **FUSOBACTERIA** also live in the intestines. They look like thin rods with pointed ends.

The intestines are also home to CYANOBACTERIA, related to water bacteria that feed on sunlight and produce oxygen. Although intestinal Cyanobacteria don't have access to sunlight and eat the same things as the others.

We need Bifidobacteria and Lactobacteria on our team.

My mom could use some of you.

Will you come with us?

MICROORGANISMS AT THE SERVICE OF HUMAN BODY

A long time ago before they even knew anything about bacteria, humans learned to use them to prepare different foods. Bacteria make cottage cheese, saurkraut, hard cheese and other products. These products are tasty, stay fresh for a long time and are good for your health. When microscopes and DNA sequencers appeared, scientists could finally figure out which microbes we are to thank for cheese, sour cream and other foods.

Let's meet them!

Let me introduce myself, Streptococcus thermophilius.

STREPTOCOCCUS THERMOPHILUS

Likes heat at the temperature of 40 degrees celcius (104 fahrenheit). It reproduces quickly arranging itself in chains and turning milk into yogurt, and then into cottage cheese and hard cheese.

LACTOBACILLUS BULGARICUS

This rod was first discovered in Bulgarian fermented milk drink and that's where it gets its name from. It is used to make yogurt, kefir, buttermilk, baked milk and other fermented milk products.

YEAST

Yeast is small fungi which live in liquids. Yeast is perhaps the most ancient microorganism tamed by man. They are used in bread baking and beer brewing. Yeast feeds on sugar and excretes carbon dioxide.

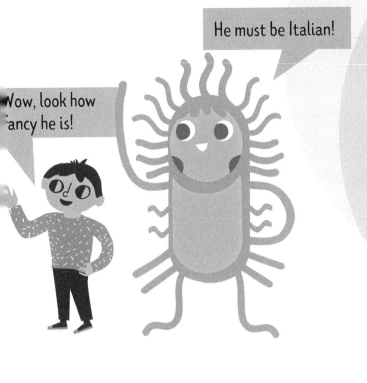

MESOPHILIC LACTIC ACID BACTERIA

Mesophilic bacteria, on the contrary, like cooler air. They are used to make hard cheeses. By the way, cheese has holes thanks to these bacteria.

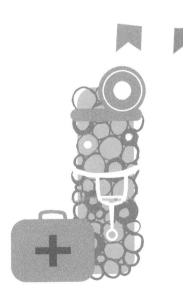

INTERESTING FACT

Ilya Mechnikov, a famous Russian-French biologist, believed that consumption of yogurt made with Lactobacillus bulgaricus may prolong your life up to a hundred years. Ilya Mechnikov was one of the first to tell people about the benefits of consumption of live culture yogurts for gut microbiota.

LACTOBACILLUS ACIDOPHILUS

This microbe was extracted by scientists from human intestines. One of its peculiarities is that once it is inside the intestines it can settle down and spread all over it. It is used to make Acidophilus milk products.

SALMONELLA ATTACK

SALMONELLA are bad bacteria that cause diseases. A person infected with Salmonella suffers from fever, dizziness, lack of energy, their stomach aches, they start vomiting and having diarrhea.

Hang on, guys!

Oh dear! We are going to be killed!

Don't let them stick to the intestinal wall!

Salmonella may get in to our body with meat, eggs and milk. They may even lurk on ordinary things touched by a sick person or animal, they can float in a pond or fly out of someone's mouth when they sneeze.

Salmonella are very treacherous and resilient bacteria and survive being frozen; they can last many days without food and even remain viable when dried out. Only heat can destroy it. That's why it's important to thoroughly cook meat, poultry, eggs and milk.

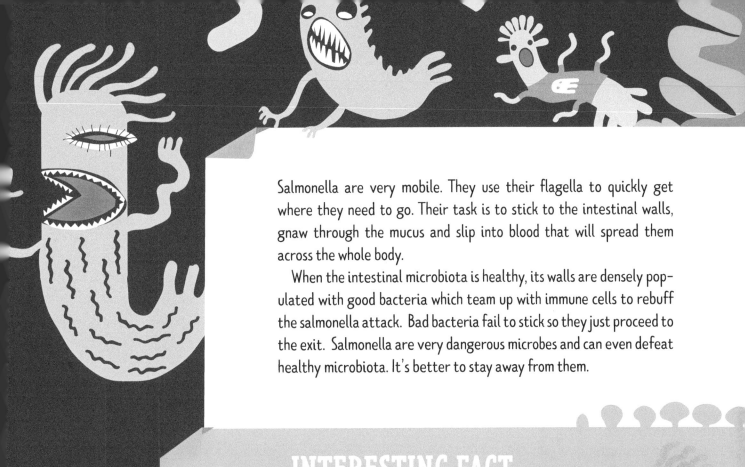

Salmonella are very mobile. They use their flagella to quickly get where they need to go. Their task is to stick to the intestinal walls, gnaw through the mucus and slip into blood that will spread them across the whole body.

When the intestinal microbiota is healthy, its walls are densely populated with good bacteria which team up with immune cells to rebuff the salmonella attack. Bad bacteria fail to stick so they just proceed to the exit. Salmonella are very dangerous microbes and can even defeat healthy microbiota. It's better to stay away from them.

INTERESTING FACT

When in 1917 Doctor Alfred Nissle treated soldiers for diarrhea he noticed that all soldiers except for one got sick. The doctor started to study microbes he took from this person and found out that his intestines had a super microbe — a special species of Escherichia coli capable of defeating illness causing microbes. To honor doctor Nissle's discovery the super microbe was called the Escherichia coli Nissle 1917. Since then it has been used to treat intestinal infections.

We have to help the good bacteria.

Call the superbacterium!

Relatives of Nissle bacteria lived in Dad's intestines. With their help good bacteria and the immunity rebuffed the Salmonella attack. Dad didn't get sick.

HORIZONTAL TRANSFER

Microbes have a superpower unlike any other complex living things. It is called the horizontal gene transfer. Bacteria can exchange pieces of DNA — genes encoding information about some of their properties or abilities.

Too bad people cannot do this. Just imagine: your friend who is great at football shook your hand and transferred to you his ability to score goals. And your karate friend shared their fighting skills. Or your dancer friend shared her talent to move gracefully. You wouldn't have to study at school for many years; you would be able to get all the knowledge you need by just shaking your teacher's hand.

Unfortunately neither humans nor animals have such abilities. We have to learn everything as well as to pass genetic information from generation to generation, like a treasure collected in small pieces.

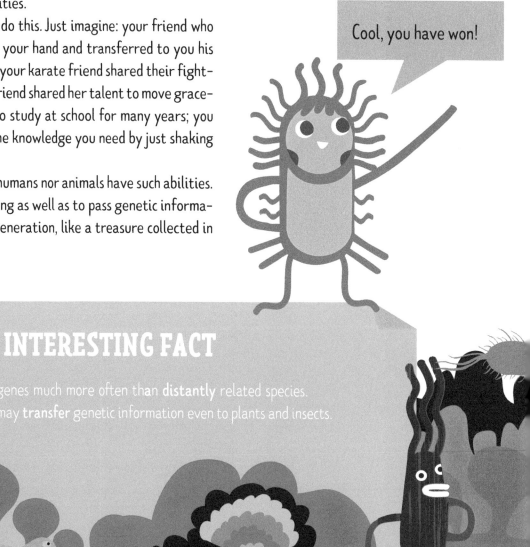

Cool, you have won!

INTERESTING FACT

Related bacteria exchange genes much more often than **distantly** related species. Nevertheless some bacteria may **transfer** genetic information even to plants and insects.

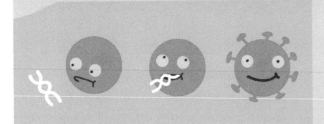

This transfer of genetic information is called horizontal transfer because it takes place between very different bacteria. Vertical transfer of genetic information is transfer of properties and abilities from parents to children.

Thanks to horizontal transfer microbes evolve much quicker than any other living things. Humans, for example, take a long time to adjust to new environments, slowly accumulating genetic changes, while microbes learn new things in a blink of an eye.

However, the ability to exchange genes is fraught with danger: bacteria may get a bad gene and start harming the human body. Or some bacteria which have a shield against antibiotics (are resistant to them) may share it with bad bacteria and then the human won't have a medicine to cure itself from illness.

The intestines have bacteria which help people to stay slim. Meet some of them. Akkermansia live on the large intestine walls deep in the mucus. They love mucus! They don't harm the intestines, just the other way around. They repair its walls by removing areas with old mucus and encouraging the intestines to produce new mucus.

Thanks to Akkermansia's work, these intestinal walls acquire a better permeability to let through nutrients and water, but can still retain bacteria. Also, Akkermansia protect us from diabetes and improve metabolism.

AKKERMANSSIA and CHRISTENSENELLA are bacteria that have been discovered recently, but have already acquired popularity. Scientists have found that lean people have more of them in their intestines than overweight people. In order to confirm this hypothesis scientists conducted an experiment: obese mice were given these bacteria with food and they lost weight.

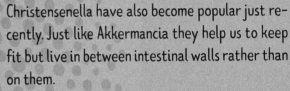

Now scientists are trying to figure out a way to use Akkermancia and Christensenella to help overweight people.

Perhaps soon, we will have probiotics with these two little bacteria and they will be prescribed to people who wish to lose weight.

Christensenella have also become popular just recently. Just like Akkermancia they help us to keep fit but live in between intestinal walls rather than on them.

Scientists found that Christensenella are inherited more often than other microbes, so the amount of these bacteria depends on how many of them your parents had. The more Christensenella are in your intestines, the better, as they prevent people from gaining excessive weight.

There are other bacteria which help us to keep fit. Like Roseburia, some Clostridia and others. They are native residents of the intestines and facilitate metabolism.

Nevertheless you should try to eat healthily. This is the easiest way to keep fit.

FARTSVILLE

Why does it smell so bad in here?

Ew! What's this stink?

Let me introduce myself, Methanobrevibacter.

Smells okay to me.

What did you say? Brevitractor?

Everyone farts. Both animals and humans. There's nothing embarrassing about it, it's healthy and even funny sometimes. However it's better not to do it in public places, like at school or at the theater, but if you can't hold it anymore, you can always go to the restroom.

But there's nothing to be ashamed of. Farting is a natural mechanism our body uses to rid itself of excessive gases. In a day you can accumulate up to a liter of gas. If you don't let it out in time, you may get a stomach ache.

Mainly farts consist of air we swallow when we eat. But some gases are produced by bacteria living in the intestines.

A gas called methane is produced by Archaea. Methanobrevibacter is the main one of them.

Methane is highly flammable, that's why you have to fart with caution near open fire. Natural gas used in stoves in our apartments is also methane. It was produced by archaea, methanobrevibacter's relatives, not in human intestines, but underground.

By the way, methane doesn't smell like anything, just like air. Farts get their distinctive smell mainly from sulfur bacteria (their scientific name is "sulfate reducing bacteria", or SRB) which excrete hydrogen sulphide that smells like rotten eggs. Some other bacteria can also produce hydrogen sulphide.

In large quantities, hydrogen sulphide is poisonous and dangerous, but in small quantities it's indispensible for our body. It helps our brain, our blood vessels and even our heart.

INTERESTING FACT

Many sulfur bacteria live in silt at the bottom of rivers, lakes, seas as well as swamps. There is a hypothesis that sulfide ore deposits appeared thanks to sulfur bacteria.

Useful Faecalibacteria also live here. They are short thin rods which cannot move. They only eat fiber and produce butyric acid which in turn feeds the intestinal wall cells. It's an exchange: we feed them and they feed our cells. These good guys monitor the intestinal health, guard the gut from inflammation, repair its walls — and protect us from illnesses caused by excessive sugar — like diabetes.

BACTERIAL RAP BATTLE

Tim and Bacteroid finished their journey insid the human body and returned to the lab. The brought a team of good superbacteria whic were supposed to help Mom get better. To tes their powers the good bacteria decided to have battle with bad bacteria that lived in a Petri dis
So the great rap battle begins! Bad bacteri versus good bacteria.

Hey, Streptococcus salivarius!
Don't mess with me,
that's just hilarious!
Spit out what you have to say,
It's nothing worth hearing anyway.

Yo!

Hey, you bad-smelling monster,
You're an evolutionary impostor.
Dental enamel eater,
humans are better off
Without you, cheater!

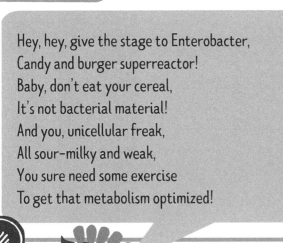

Hey, hey, give the stage to Enterobacter,
Candy and burger superreactor!
Baby, don't eat your cereal,
It's not bacterial material!
And you, unicellular freak,
All sour-milky and weak,
You sure need some exercise
To get that metabolism optimized!

We are Bifidobacteria!
Bad microbes don't meet our criteria!
My lactate is worse than any attack,
Surrender and maybe I'll cut you some slack!
We don't need this drama,
Go run to E.coli a.k.a. your momma!
Your DNA can say "Adieu",
I'd neutralize it before you split in two.

91

MOM'S RECOVERY

I found good bacteria for Mom. Will you make some medicine with them?

I wonder where you found them.

This method of treatment is called
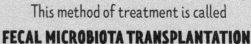
FECAL MICROBIOTA TRANSPLANTATION

Transplantation of microbes from a healthy person is a new method of treatment studied by microbiologists all over the world. Is it possible to transplant good microbes to a sick person to treat them for inflammation and intestinal infection, stomach ache and feeling unwell? Experiments tell us it is.

Microbiota transplantation works the same way as probiotics: the intestines are populated with good microbes which increase its ability to resist bad ones. The only difference is that a whole community of microbes is transplanted, which means there are more chances that good bacteria will settle down.

In order to collect the good bacteria from the intestines, we need to have a person poop into a jar with a special solution. That's right, good microbes are taken from feces of a healthy person. Then microbiota is thoroughly studied in the lab, rinsed and cleansed. When only good microbes are left, they are placed in the sick person's intestines.

Another way is to place good bacteria into a capsule, which will take them to the sick person's intestines. That's exactly what Tim's dad did. Mom took the medicine and the next day she started feeling better. Soon the doctors let her go home. Tim was so happy that for a moment he forgot that he'll never see his friend Bacteroid again.

After a special dinner to celebrate Mom's return, Tim put his ear to Mom's belly and started listening. Something was bubbling and mysteriously humming inside. He remembered his friends who were busy settling down in new cities inside Mom's belly.

MICR-R-R-ROBIOTA!

Tim's Adventures in the World of Bacteria
Copyright 2019 by Dmitry Alexeev

Published by Piscataqua Press
32 Daniel St., Portsmouth, NH 03801

info@piscataquapress.com

ISBN: 978-1-950381-26-5

9 781950 381265